I had 1  .

one box

I had 2 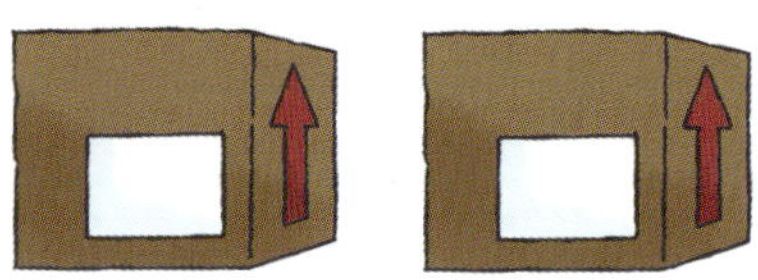 .

two boxes

Boxes

by Quin Reed
illustrated by Joss Reegan

Practice Pre-Decodable 9

McGraw Hill Education

Bothell, WA • Chicago, IL • Columbus, OH • New York, NY

MHEonline.com

Send all inquiries to:
McGraw-Hill Education
8787 Orion Place
Columbus, OH 43240

ISBN: 978-0-02-140451-3
MHID: 0-02-140451-8

Printed in the United States of America.

8 9 10 CTM 23

I had 3 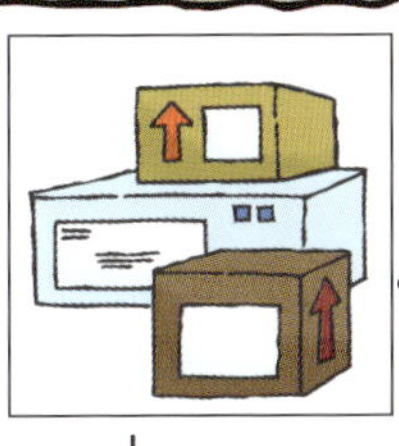 .

three boxes

I had 4 .

four boxes

I had  .

five boxes

I had 0  .

zero boxes